American Ghost Roses

## Books by Kevin Stein

Poetry
> *American Ghost Roses* (2005)
> *Chance Ransom* (2000)
> *Bruised Paradise* (1996)
> *A Circus of Want* (1992)

Criticism
> *Private Poets, Worldly Acts* (1996)
> *James Wright, The Poetry*
> *of a Grown Man* (1989)

Anthology
> *Illinois Voices*, edited with
> G. E. Murray (2001)

# American Ghost Roses

## *Poems by* KEVIN STEIN

University of Illinois Press
*Urbana and Chicago*

1 2 3 4 5 C P 5 4 3 2 1

Library of Congress Cataloging-in-Publication Data
Stein, Kevin, 1954–
American ghost roses : poems / by Kevin Stein.
p.   cm. — (Illinois poetry series)
ISBN 0-252-02998-4 (cloth : acid-free paper)
ISBN 0-252-07240-5 (pbk. : acid-free paper)
I. Title. II. Series.
PS3569.T3714A83     2005
811'.54—dc22     2005002014

# Acknowledgments

Several poems in this manuscript have appeared previously. Grateful acknowledgment is made to the following magazines:

*Boulevard:* "Adolescent Hemlock," "Instructor's Comments on the Poem 'Eden Sleeping,' Circa 1975," and "Love Poem with Knife and Last-Cut Zinnia." *Colorado Review:* "Superstitious Manna." *Crab Orchard Review:* "Found in a Shoe Box Labeled 'Keep.'" *The Kenyon Review:* "Upon Witnessing My Mother Impossibly Blossom above My Father's Death Bed" and "Wishful Rhetoric." *Meridian:* "Tract." *The North American Review:* "Windfall." *The North Dakota Quarterly:* "Upon Blowing Our Chance to Meet the Poet Laureate, Who's Probably a Nice Guy" and "Valentine's Day Boxing at the Madison County Jail." *Ontario Review:* "In the House of Being" and "Revelation in Pinks and Red." *Poet Lore:* "The Cost." *Poetry East:* "Sappho's Fragment 63." *River Styx:* "How He Answered the Glossy Magazine's *Mate-Poaching* Survey." *The Southern Review:* "An American Tale of Sex and Death." *Sou'wester:* "To Wheelbarrows." *Tampa Review:* "Thinking of Kandinsky while Shaving My Father." *TriQuarterly:* "Reintroductions" and "To the Reader Awakened by a Noisy Furnace."

"Ghosts" is for Dean Young and Fleeta Lacomara+. "An American Tale of Sex and Death" is in memory of Clayton Nunn.

I'm grateful for support offered by Bradley University, which granted me time to write some of these poems. For plentiful advice and encouragement, I am indebted to Keith Ratzlaff, Jeff Gundy, Clint McCown, and Dean Young. Thanks also to Teeven, Fuller, and Crowe for that bridge and the woods beyond. Thanks to Jimmy's welcome diversion. Thanks to Mara, Lily, and Flash for beauty of spirit and motion. Thanks to Deb whose love sustains, her shovel and ladder, her blossoms and their fruit. Thanks to Kirsten and Joseph for their gift of becoming. Thanks to Annie Wright for hers and his.

*In memory of Joseph Stein,*
*for Mary Rita Stein*

# Contents

## One

Wishful Rhetoric   *3*

## Two

To the Reader Awakened by a Noisy Furnace   *7*

An American Tale of Sex and Death   *9*

Reintroductions   *13*

Adolescent Hemlock   *15*

In the House of Being   *17*

The Cost   *22*

Revelation in Pinks and Red   *23*

Superstitious Manna   *25*

Kandinsky's *Concerning the Spiritual in Art*   *26*

Windfall   *29*

Upon Witnessing My Mother Impossibly Blossom
above My Father's Deathbed   *30*

## Three

Love Poem with Knife and Last Cut Zinnia   *35*

Sappho's Fragment 63   *38*

Instructor's Comments on the Poem
"Eden Sleeping," Circa 1975   *40*

How He Answered the Glossy Magazine's
*Mate-Poaching* Survey   *42*

Upon Blowing Our Chance to Meet the
Poet Laureate, Who's Probably a Nice Guy   *44*

Etiquette and Epiphany in the
Post-Workshop Men's Room   *46*

The Other One   *48*

To Bob Marley's Toe   *50*

Ghosts   *52*

To Bananas   *54*

Reliquary   *56*

Four

Thinking of Kandinsky while
Shaving My Father   *61*

Theory & Practice   *63*

Valentine's Day Boxing at the
Madison County Jail   *65*

Found in a Shoe Box Labeled "Keep"   *70*

In the Nuclear Age   *74*

Upon Freeing the Ruby-Throated Hummingbird
Beak-Stuck in a Screen Door   *76*

To Wheelbarrows   *78*

While Writing This Poem, My Horse
Jumped the Pasture Fence   *80*

These Gifts   *82*

Won't You Stand Next to My Fire   *84*

Tract   *86*

"The spirit, like the body, can be strengthened and developed by frequent exercise. . . . The artist must train not only his eye but also his soul."

—Wassily Kandinksy

"The times I burned my guitar it was like a sacrifice. You sacrifice the things you love."

—Jimi Hendrix

# One

# Wishful Rhetoric

*Finis.* I love the oh-so-postmodern opening—
the reversal of expectations intimating a fresh start,
as does potty-training or the pre-dinner after-dinner mint.
After all, in this way the end's a beginning.

So *Finis.* There now, the daisies' clean faces
need never wrinkle, their eyes never shut,
and the plump clump swaying in May breeze
need never dismantle June's skeletal erector set.

That's that. So the orchard's Jonathan need not
drop and rot, the iris's plush petals might
always enshrine its flushed lips, and the lilac
(my favorite) can spend its profligate scent

without fear of overdraft. Breathe in and forget
the out. I am the bank, the root, the fat honeycomb.
I am the aphid milking an everlasting tit.
There now, I'll make the twenty calls from home,

each beginning, "My father died last night."

# Two

Depressing + Disturbing, Nostalgioc

# To the Reader Awakened by a Noisy Furnace

You've heard the one about the two-bit crook
    who, when fingered for the cops, spills all. He sings,
they say, like a canary, and thus avoids jail. As does his boss,
    who whispers "In God We Trust" in a few open palms.

In time the guy finds decent work in another city.
    He settles into domesticity, until one winter
*poof,* he's gone. Come spring, fishermen haul up their catch—
    a corpse without head or hands, face or fingerprints.

Well, what of the dictator, little matter which, plush
    among the palms and many-fingered dates,
who so hates to hear a complaint, even the silent language
    of the deaf, he will not have it. No, no, no.

So when the *dissident,* a plump word for so thin a man,
    asks for sleeping mats, a generous gruel,
some pencils for the boys to scrawl on banana leaf,
    the big man, the fat man, the sovereign

can't fathom the insult. Abashed, he whispers in a curled
    attentive ear, and the deed is as he wished.
Still, the thin man, the man who speaks with his hands
    won't shut up—even with each finger lopped

off by bolt cutting shears. Sure, silence blankets
    each marble step while the stitches heal
and the new moon raises its scimitar. Then the thin man,
    the deaf man whumps the stumps of his palms

like a drum, and the beat speaks a word, grunt and anthem
    even his ears can hear. And you, reading this
snug in your downy bed, the furnace thumping its thump,
    you hear it too, or something very like it.

*Adressing Reader* [handwritten annotation]

And now when it thumps again, you'll think not of that
    but of this—the petty crook and the innocent
dissident—how language like a song cost one his life,
    and song like language gave the other his back.

Or sort of. You'll fester there beneath the sheets,
    thinking my story's all wrong, aghast at its
skewed mix of guilt and innocence, word and silence.
    Perhaps then you'll think this the stitch

to thread these both, and money's hand in each,
    and think the storyteller, yes, me,
is some moon-eyed Marxist on relief. Simmer down.
    Be patient. The furnace ought soon click off.

When it doesn't, you'll stumble up in slippers
    and trip on your sleeping yellow dog
in route to notch it gentle down, gas prices on the rise.
    Back in bed, all three of us, yes—you'll feel

but not see the deaf man and me—the three of us
    will curse and blow in what hands we have:
a cold hand that says or does any human thing,
    the rueful hand that writes it down.

8

# An American Tale of Sex and Death

*Taboo subjects*
*Look truth in the eye or your blind*

Before I'd felt the promised kiss of either—
pink tongue of one, feathered breath of the other—
*sex*                              *death*
I knew their kinship among lords of life
*look up*
and fealty I'd pay from pocket or heart,
or both. Stoic Catholic teacher-priests
had ceded the subject to shocked locker
room gossip, so imagine my wonder,
child of the fat book, when I blundered on
*Romeo and Juliet* in the library
*analogy*
Carnegie's steel monopoly gifted
my Hoosier town. Oh how the bard's language
spilled like sunlight through the oft-zitted dome
*simile*   *fresh, immature*
shrouding my green teenage brain, a verbal
hubbub above the flesh and brash sword play.

☾    ☾    ☾

Our play at home featured yardstick-duels,
my sister trilling, "Avaunt, arrant knave"
until I thwacked her knuckles and she cried.
Sent to my room, I bled Mercutio's       *metaphor/allusion*
last gasp into red carpet, perfecting
the raised head's fall. By luck, Zeffirelli's
classic movie remake graced the downtown
Paramount's sagging screen. It cost a week's
lunch money, glad fasting, so friends and I
might treat a sweet trio of girls beneath
the balcony's stiff lip. I'd love to say
our hand-holding, like any gateway drug,

led to higher pleasures, but mine was greased
with popcorn slurb and hers was wet with sweat.

*imagery*

        (       (       (

Don't sweat the truth: It wasn't my heart's first
nor last diffident failure, and this time
I looked up when Olivia Hussey's
olive chest splashed on screen, each breast maybe
four feet across and deeply cleaved. Though I'd
seen others flashed in sticky magazines     *refrencing boys but used*
flooring the burned-out basement where bad boys   *the far alliteration*
sniffed glue, and though since I've held love's ample
gifts, none was as monstrously glorious   *oxymoron*
as these Shakespeare conjured in serif type.
Who was Capulet and who Montague
I don't remember, nor the actor's name
who played Romeo in stitched elastic
tights, that too-prissy narcissistic fool.   *conceited*   *diction*

        (       (       (

We three fools of brushed velour mourned those breasts
amidst the climax's sad collapse. Moping
and hushed, we walked our brick streets home, the girls
safely station-wagoned off by mommy. *diction*
That not one of us boys had touched any
sweatered breast meant not a lick. Confusion
fueled our hormonal musings, April '68,
a few ticks late for the Summer of Love
we'd read about soundly after the fact.
A crowd frothed around the YMCA,
someone with a yellow bullhorn lathered
the night faces that dipped and rose like waves
of inland seas. When we turned on Lincoln,
the bullhorn's feedback asked, *Hey, what's the time?*

                        ☾        ☾        ☾

The time's answer: One fist smashed my glasses,
another my white cheek. Each swing brought its
own brass-knuckled reply: "Time for Dr. King,"
"Time for our Miss Rosa," "My time, mo-fo"—
each quick punch a blunt, punctuated grunt.
I rope-a-doped as would Ali in his
Thrilla in Manila, till each had done
with me what he would. The yellow bullhorn
bellowed, *What's the time?* The brothers answered,
*Black Power, Black Power,* until I knew
what it was to have none. In dewy grass,          *imagery*
beneath a sappy maple, I looked in
their eyes and they in mine. All right, we looked
but didn't—this, the day Martin got his.

                        ☾        ☾        ☾

His was death, though I'd like to say I learned
a fleshed lesson—one you carry folded
in the pocket your wallet's in, something
to mull in traffic, awaiting the doc,
or popping corn for the rented movie
the kids can't watch. You're waiting to hear it,
white America, so you can smirk your
absolution. And yes, you're waiting too,
black America, so you can shake your head,
I don't get it. When the twenty finished
with me, they chanted down Lincoln's rubble.
One man, eyeing my near-sighted fumble
and plea, picked up my too thick black-rimmed specs
and placed them gently on my swollen face.          *immagery*

                        ☾        ☾        ☾

"Face it, you at the wrong place at the wrong
time, brother." He said *brother*. Through cracked lens,
we might've been—his face pieced together
as Picasso knew before the first war,
before the second, before Jeanie Creek
tended my lumps, she pregnant by a black
guy her parents wouldn't let her marry.
Her radio spun the web we're trapped in,
as Zombies sang "it's the time of the season
for loving." My friend Clayton, black as his name,
kicked the gang leader's butt. For me, he said.
I looked in his eyes, he in mine. America?
Sure: Clayton's in prison, I write sonnets.
The truth? Look it in the eye or you're blind.

# Reintroductions

*Actually black in color, indigo buntings have no*
*blue pigment. The diffraction of light through the*
*structure of their wings makes them appear blue.*

"Sweet Mother of God," the curse wings fire
from a man whose hand's been slammed
in his truck door, his language blue and wounded—
as was the Virgin herself, blue not only in sadness
but also in dress, her robes a color not unlike these
indigo buntings we're returning to the flood plain
farmed thirty years by a salt magnate now gone,
his dirt levy, too. Nothing much grew here.
The silt's gift sifted only an inch or two,
then sand, Illinois River rock, and tax write-offs.
The almighty buck. I'm lucky enough
to be here because I know a guy who knows
the Ranger whose smashed hand lit blue flame,
so I say "sir" a lot, nodding to the park's
khaki Lancelot of the plastic fold-up table.
Our chivalry's redundant at 5 A.M.,
as all acts of love come pursed in darkness
or shadow, penumbra of the soul. Did I say all?

Around us, spring peepers give forth their chorus
of hours, each day an eon in heavenly sway,
each coupling stirring the froth of back    *consonance?*
and forth, this world and not. I want to believe,
and believing's mostly want. And though    *inversion of sentence order*
it's not extinction we're making extinct here—
only a rift in earth's silk stocking—I'm sappy

daft enough to trundle a boom box that loops
the birds' digitized warble to calm and comfort them,
each phrase and note repeated to calm and comfort.
In cages draped with oven-warmed towels,
these birds must think we're gods or fools.
Ah, yes. Maybe it's the nothing we're filling
with wings, or these wings that rise on nothing.
Maybe the blue that's really black, the blue
that isn't. Whatever lifts this occasion begs
the reintroduction of me to me, eye to eye,

though who am I to me? The question lingers
a lifetime, which is to say, till death—the moment
of knowing also our last. Or not-knowing,
also our last. I am waiting still, meaning *calm,*
and still meaning *yet.* I am both and nothing,
both nothing and the press of air against flesh.
I am despot and savior, I am cynic and dreamer.
I am the boy at the door and the door locked
on him. I am the one who dutifully records
the day's time, temperature, and wind speed.
I am the one who forgets his No. 2 pencil.
I am the buntings black in low scrub.
I am the sunlight that flames them sudden
iridescent blue. I am the one who makes
the introductions: Birds, this is your world.
World, these are your kin. Amen.
I am the one who's turned away
when the cage door's flung open.

# Adolescent Hemlock

Say you're 16 and your mother's dying in
spoonfuls of custard frosted around its edge
by your avocado refrigerator
green as the eyes she's dying in,
so while you're there you squeeze in
some Plochman's mustard yellow as the skin
she's dying in, and pitiless Vivaldi offers
endless winter because the turntable's needle
rides the carpet of dust we'll all become,
and since from dust ye came, you add a pinch
from the floor's corner the mop won't reach
when she kicks the bucket she's dying in
while redbuds shed their tousled blooms
as she does her hair, so you fist in
dropped blossoms for the color her cheeks
used to be, though at 16 you leave
things open as the bed she's dying in,
pink sheets and daisies, so petals and pollen
lend the blender a festive note as you ladle in
Liquid Drano—one cup, two—and press puree.

Say your mother's already half down
the drain, and your sodden father's passed out
upon the couch, and your footfalls fill
the small hall her bedroom spills in.
Say the mug's beneficence brims
its grim grin—this kindness, her letting go.
Say you give a shiver when guilt trills

15

its little a cappella in your seashell ear, *metaphor* *rhyming*
so it's 1-2 a gulp for you, 3-4 down some more,
5-6 you'll get sick, 7-8 accept your fate, *suicide*
9-10 the end begins. Say the shocked doc's
plastic shunt salvages your burnt gullet.
Say a nurse hunts the beaded string she's looped *Anaphora continued*
through your nose, throat, gut, and out
so your airway won't scar shut. Say you die
but don't. Say you dream then what you've dreamed
before: frosh gym, and Mr. Wooden splinters *irony?*
his voice poking you up the knotted rope.
For once no snickers, no jock itch, not a single
twitch or bead of sweat. Say the air's as hushed
as the hospital waiting room. Say this time—
no, next—you'll reach the top knot's heaven.

# In the House of Being

## I

Not why, though something as perilous and perilously close
    I'd wanted to ask
my teenage pal who'd gulped down Drano while his mother
    lay dying with cancer.
He'd lived, if living is what you make of what remains,
    the bulk of you there
but something bored clean and gone, a hole like that *Oh*
    the lips shape
when someone punches your belly and wind whooshes out,
    your next breath
arriving on the late plane from Memphis with news the King
    is dead.
Long live rock 'n' roll. Though he wore survivors' shocked look,
    and wore too,
I realize now, a colostomy bag to catch the meager crap
    his intestines couldn't
(no doubt the reason he sat out gym), he seemed the guy
    I always knew,
save for the platinum beaded string looped through his nose,
    throat, gut and out
somewhere above the belt so it swung up and in his right nostril.
    In school
his pass dismissed him before the rest so he might snake
    this beaded string
through pinched aperture of throat and gut. If it scarred shut,
    he'd be fed by vein.

Or else. Once, blundering in a fetid restroom stall,
  flushed
with the flu, I caught that ritual's last twist before he buttoned
  his button-down
and my urge to retch had been strangely quelled.

## II

At twelve we played summer ball for Norris Quality Cars,
  cheap auto lot
blighting Fifth Street's rat end. Tall and thin, *a long drink of water*
  parents called him,
he lurked about first base with the supple, slow-motion grace
  of the white crane.
Nothing got by him. Not the line shot or any high and wide
  I hurled
from deep short to prove my arm a gun, the ball our secret
  heard
only when his mitt popped. That easy. Then the raised fist,
  a cheer,                                    *onomotopeia*
the ball whipped around the horn *whump, whump, whump.*
  In the grandstand,
his mother was a wisp in sundress and bonnet, her voice
  the feather
in his ear, calling "Way to go" or "Atta boy, Dan," something
  sibilant and sheltered
amidst his father's hissing "Five bucks, kiddo," fist parading
  a wadded Lincoln.
Every time he came to bat, cash money was on the line.
  In after-game gloaming,
teams would string a line for fountain Coke, Sprite, cream soda,
  or the "suicide" – *connection to previous poem*
that mixed all three, a bubbly concoction colored as nothing
  in nature.

Each time she'd stand with him and talk, her bonnet's brim
        lightly touching
his ball cap's brim. The other parents huddled by their cars,
        ignored and ignoring,
until we boys stumbled darkly among the assembled Chevies,
        succumbing,
at dusk, to ride home with the strangers we'd made of them.

*Not appreciating Parents*

## III

Not why, not that exactly, still something akin I'd have liked
        to ask him,
even though I feared he'd answer *why not?* and then what
        fool American thing
would I have blurted: JFK, Billy Graham, Richard Nixon
        before the fall?
He was less of this place than anyone I knew. Before either
        of us could drive,
his father's black Porsche squealed halt at my parents' place
        hard by the tracks,
the proverbial tracks, and they drove me over our usual river
        up Van Buskirk hill
to his brick house ridge top obscured by vintage oaks.
        Dan stacked albums
and cranked it up: Mozart, first I'd heard, then Beethoven
        for beginners,
his Fifth, and just for kicks The William Tell Overture
        whose cannons
we bottomed by thudding basketballs against the wall.
        Then photos
of Europe, Dan in tan lederhosen, too many forks beside
        the plate,
and a black maid I answered "Yes, ma'am" so often
        everyone

laughed at me. In truth I wanted to go home to Motown
    on my radio,
The Beatles on LP, my mother's meat loaf browning
    her Spic and Span oven. *brand?*
In truth I wanted to ask him not why but why Drano?
    Instead,
hostage to what language cannot say, tongue-tied guest
    in Heidegger's
House of Being, I plunged words' blue blade into his chest,
    "Why's
that fucking string in your nose?" I walked home alone.

## IV

Not why but *why not,* you must've thought, your mother dying
    in spoonfuls
of frosted custard—slow, slow—the spoon a knife in your hand.
    Whose heart?
Maybe you thought first of her release, maybe she asked if not
    with words
then with her eyes. What tool for such a thing does a boy have?
    What hand?
Because your dad's a shrink—that bitter pill—he locks his silver
    medicine chest
as the cops suggest, though beneath the sink there's this and that.
    Whose lips?
Mixing your elixir, the room must've filled with sun, as if
    the answer arrived
dressed in gowns of light. Or maybe the dark crept up
    behind you,
no matter the hour, its cloak tight about your shoulders
    as a wizard
might shroud his secret potion. In your walk there was sound,
    in the sound a word

knocking no, no, no against your ear's locked door.
    Whose life?
Not hers. So you drank it quick, a way to say what
    you couldn't,
awaiting its furtive verdict in the word *Goodbye*
    which came,
at last, in twin fists of *Hello* and *Welcome back*. Alas.
    And though
you shook it off, finished school, got a job—
    isn't that
what real Americans do?, buck up, good buddy!—
    it's also true
your self-hate made you finally one of us.

# The Cost

"Top drawer on the right," my father yells,
too shaky to screw himself out of the chair,
his Parkinson's a blight today, so I shovel
for the checkbook to pay an overdue bill
he's misplaced and then simply forgotten.
There, in his underwear drawer, buried
beside the pistol, beneath private cotton,
there's the single yellow envelope scrawled
in his schoolboy's hand, "Mary Francis's hair."
One golden curl clipped from the kid sister
askew in mother's arms, rheumatic fever,
dead before '29's crash—in those old days
back when there was no cure, as there's none now,
my friends, to quell this ache. Love makes us pay.

# Revelation in Pinks and Red

No one knew till she was ten, climbing black oak to snatch the hanging basket orioles stitched to a branch. Reaching she slip-dropped on Hardin's wrought iron fence and pierced the chest where her heart should've been but wasn't. She hung there, 55 lbs. surprised child, feet two feet above the snow. Valentine's cold stanched the flow till Hardin *oxymoron* came home for bagel, banana, and fifteen carrot sticks sliced fresh each day, oh comfort of routine, this time to find a girl impaled on his fence beneath the tree where orioles nest. TV arrived as firemen laddered her gently off, asking mama was there trouble for skipping school. Newspapers declaimed, "The Girl with Her Heart on the Wrong Side." Kids called her the human pincushion or Darth Vader whose heart crossed over to the dark side. *Contemporary Allusion*

Her fifteen minutes faded to zits and algebra tutors, cross her *irony* heart and hope to die, though saying the Pledge she put her hand on the right side and a teacher said that's wrong but of course the right was right not left. She took a hostess job after her CC degree in restaurant management, and the few she slept with, hammerers of nail in wood, rolled their tongues over the scar until she felt like a circus geek. They put an ear to her flushed chest—some disgusted, some aroused by the wrong-sided whoosh as others favor a limp or crossed glass eye. In defense her poems came in fits and spells, though the social service shrink who'd pop his gum all through their weekly thirty loved most the one which strung a child above miles of red snow, exaggeration a gift she was born with, as was her heart on the wrong side. Three summers at artists' colony, and the painter she'd crushed on came out gay, thus safe, so she let him paint her nude

*Poems are like trains of thought*

23

from the waist up, a series entitled *The Woman with Her Heart on the Right Side,* featuring two nipples, a raised scar, and one red X to mark the spot.

# Superstitious Manna

Face down, a good luck penny becomes the bad
no one will touch. On the cakewalk sidewalk,
copper beacon of promise gone wrong,
its glint begs "Pick me up," a hint of mischief
in the way light puddles against its thin brim,
nearly spilling but not. Folks sidestep around,
as they would any black cat breaking a mirror
on Friday the 13th. For you it winks "I'm yours,"
so sweetly you hear coins clink in the piggy bank
whose nose you ballpeened off to buy
an Easter kite April maples got the best of.  *euphamism*
Now *Loss and Redemption,* and not the Easter story's,
but your own kid's kite caught and just set free

at Main & University on a Monday noon
halfway through your fifth decade—the circle
of chance come home at last. Well, perhaps.
Sappho, who knew a thing or two of breakage,
warned *don't disturb the rubble.* When you crank
your bad back toward it, a world's weight rests
on you, Atlas of the middle-aged. What gift
have you the sense to refuse? What kiss
on cheek or lips? There's shimmering Lincoln
enthroned in the penny's pint-sized memorial,
dead for his cause. "Touch me," he coos,
though who would dare but you, the child
whose mother smacked your hand, "Dirty, dirty."

*Poems connect to eachother and back to themselves*

# Kandinsky's *Concerning the Spiritual in Art*

Barry's father worked with bruise as Kandinsky did with chalk,
    knuckling punch
over punch so blood shone through his mother's skin as sunlight
    through stained glass. *violent disturbing mood*
With cruelty, like most drugs, eventually you need more to get off:
    another line,
the needle, one more hit to frill the bruise like red wine bled
    on Irish doily.
In shadowed sleeve he worked, beneath blouse or skirt high
    on the thigh,
her body the canvas of his private demon. His priest asked Barry
    to beseech
the Body of Christ, wafer of peace and penance, to bestow
    his father
the leaven bread of redemption. Instead he took karate lessons.
    He kicked
his father's not-so-sorry ass. In the bruised blue aftermath,
    dad packed *zeugma*
bottle and wife in a rusted Plymouth Duster the color
    of split lip, *imagery that relates*
valve lifters tick ticking, the bomb headed for Kentucky
    where
a man could do what he wanted to what he owned,
    "Screw the soul."

Whose art answers that, Kandinsky? Whose apt hand sketches
    the "strivings of the soul"

you spoke of, just before the war to end all wars didn't? *irony*
    However muddled,
our art blushed the other cheek with booze, sink light
    elbowing
its low-watt corona across the kitchen's paint-by-number
    Mt. Rushmore.
American heroes. Well, one of us. Zit-faced and shit-faced,
    we sang the blues.
My voice cracked like eagle shell thinned by DDT, so what
    burst forth
wasn't winged beauty. Barry cranked up his Vox amp
    and plucked the Fender
with vigor—"Be the key," he pleaded. I chortled, flat
    as the veined knobs
protruding from my half-human neck. His neighbors' pajamas,
    armed with the flaming torch
of a cop's flashlight, turned me off with one quick flipped switch:
    "Yes, officer."

Make what you will of the cops' stopping my wailing but not hers. *irony*
    Make what you will
of history's middle finger: a girl's Hiroshima shadow, her teaspoon
    of dust.
Make what you will of eyes where ears ought to be, toe-jam
    in tank tread.
What numbers paint that face? My voice can't wake the dead. *father*
    Neither will oil on canvas
nor this poem. It's spirit not spire, Kandinsky, body of belief
    the hand can't touch.
For you, art is "the child of its time, mother of our emotions."
    Put a fist to that.
Or this: Barry's mother lasted five years in a Kentucky shack.
    She never came back.

*You can't physically hurt words*

Shack rhymes with back and so with smack but not with soul.
    That night
we learned the fine art of the bruise. Vinegar with oil.
    That night
we gulped scotch from Tupperware cups. Upchuck in a sink.
    That night his fist
painted what soul he could: 5 blue, 3 green, 2 yellow 2 yellow,
    1 black eye between us.

# Windfall

When some plump apple plops in wet grass
it's not <u>Newton</u> I remember, late September
wind and sideways rain, though gravity
drops one body atop another just so. Just so.
Not William Tell or the son his arrow loved
less than he, nor Johnny Appleseed sporting
on his head a soup pot the Tell kid could've put
to good use. Neither our underpaid teachers
nor the brown-nosed students who pester them
with purblind kindness, nor all the doctors
kept at bay by daily grace of Jonathan, Cortland,
Red Delicious, the Macintosh that won't compute.

If you gamble, odds are you're betting it's Eve
I've in mind, but no, not that story either.
Never bet against the house, even one made of cards.
Listen, falling's a lesson Sappho learned in bed
and bath, waking as her towel dropped morning.
I love how her fragments fell to us on shards
of terra cotta, papyrus strips stuffed in mouths
of mummified crocodiles, or the few tensile lines
quoted by Plutarch, Aristotle, Longinus
for grammar and felicity of heart. Shall I say it?
Though we've only Sappho's windfall apple,
we've thus her blossom, fruit, and seed.

*allusions*

*- all relate to apples*

29

# Upon Witnessing My Mother
# Impossibly Blossom above
# My Father's Deathbed


Creek creek, the floor says, like water through
      oak woods. Creak creak, it says, little strokes
fell great oaks. She leans to him as the red rose

leans in sudden storm. Franklin says a word
      to the wise breaks your mother's back.
No, a needle a day keeps the doctor away.

Clouds say April showers bring big weeds.
      Today loose lips break my mother's back,
so she bends over him as day folds over night.

"Rita," his voice creaks, "water." Yes,
      a stitch in time breaks your mother's back,
meaning they saved him but from what cliff?

Sure, a beer a day makes a man healthy,
      wealthy, and wise, though when the well's dry,
you come to know the worth of water.

He whispers in her ear, begging to leave home
      for home. And what of his black cats?
For want of a nail, the hoarse floor creaks.

So she fluffs his pillow, adjusts the blinds,
      and blankets the word no one will say.
Step on a crack and lose your horse shoe.

30

Now she presses the button that brings
    May flowers and his head up for soup.
Spoons sink ships, loose lips sink soup.

Lifting him she grunts like a soul trucker.
    Little strokes say creek creek, clouds say water,
water says peace upon his lips. Creak creak,

his oak grove groans in blackberry breeze.
    Speak now, my son, or forever count your chickens.
Say, for want of a shovel we plant in the clouds.

# Three

More random, less morbid

# Love Poem with Knife and Last Cut Zinnia

After the crocus lifts its chalice and the tulip's blushed cup
    spills ambrosia,
after the American Beauty folds its tent and poppy's orange
    betrays its black eye,
long after delphinium and veronica mimic sky, after the astilbe
    weaves its lace
among blue lupine gone purple, after liatris spikes white
    then topples
and the lilies' day becomes night, after the phlox' flame
    burns its glad match—
right then, at the trilogy's last emphatic sentence,
    zinnia preside,
queens of unbecoming coming on, long-necked blooms
    stretched above
splotched greenery, lair of the spider, a moth hung there
    in hungry light,
quivering repose before the repose. Sleep tight.

Because nothing's subtle about October, I don't want
    to die—
candles aflame, that little tent, flowers and shovels slick
    with rain—
though surely this day bears seduction inevitable as the lover's
    champagne glance,
raspberry beret tossed atop the bedpost we tumbled across
    and in,

in and out of this world seductive as sunlight webbed
        with dew.
Because I never put to memory Bryant's "Thanatopsis"
        as Sister Carmencita
wished me to. Because I heard but didn't listen to
        Father Kay
pray as he oiled grandma's temples as if with dew.
        Because the whole
boatload from Zen to Catholicism rocks broken-hulled
        on the shores
of Now-This, that seduction, I'll admit something
        hungers for us
we can't imagine being swallowed by, a notion
        we can't fathom
on days we're not the Dalai Lama. Say, today.

So we'll stop to haul the turtle across Highway 46,
        flip open the screen
a Dragon fly clings to, eat Red Delicious, jog miles
        against
the traffic's head shakes. We want to live forever
        webbed with sunlight
and dew. Because they say love tastes honeyed
        after a fight
when making out smacks of making up, let's lie.
        Let's say the fight
we never had had everything to do with zinnia,
        because in truth
it would've. Come risk my whiskers and stale bagel breath.
        Bend with me
on knee before the zinnia May offers October's dross.
        Let's pluck the moth
and thwart the spider, skew the seasonal happenstance,
        the week's bleak theater.

Let's mouth the <u>hour</u>'s round <u>bower</u> of <u>vowels</u>
    these zinnia sing
before hoar frost—A E I Oh You, oh you, again—
    kiss me.
You whose tongue cleaves deep as any knife.

*Smile*

Look up

# Sappho's Fragment 63

The shard of terra cotta,

  beloved but broken

   at some age or another,

 says only

*a dripping towel.*

  Still Sappho catches

   gravity's apple,

  the seed within,

as a fall

  frees beauty from branch

 to lips,

the way my love

  steps from the shower

   wrapped in a towel

gravity will have its way

with,

and thus

the Winesap,

Honey Crisp,

Golden Delicious,

the sharp cheddar and parsley

her body is.

Form -falling

*Similar to Borges* [handwritten]

# Instructor's Comments on the Poem
# "Eden Sleeping," Circa 1975

*look up* [handwritten]

When you claim "God stays up late to watch
the insomniac poet scrawl" his *clunky syntax*
"masterpiece in praise of sleep," I applaud.
*Taut irony,* though *awkward,* hereafter *awk.*
The part about the apple carrying "its seeds
as a woman schleps her fetus" shows *dry wit*
until deer eat the fruit of knowledge.
*Surreal image! Beware of tense shifts.*
When the "natural digestive process" creates
*line break* "man and woman from dung,"
the poem drops to the scatological. *Tighten.*
This may offend the sensibilities of those
who'd otherwise enjoy *understatement* Hamlet
"budding from the garden's infamous tree."
*Who's speaking here? Have you read Keats?*
Though there's something *deft allusion* "rotten"
in the state of Denmark, one wouldn't,
as you say, "nip it in the bud." *Recast.*
This *mixed metaphor* is reminiscent of Castlereagh,
subject of my father's *nice, very nice* dissertation.
Know thyself, says Socrates, or soon you'll ask,
Would you like fries with that? *I'm lost.*
*Are you?* Of your aversion to punctuation,
I say *Make it new!* Do you smoke pot?
*Yes, yes.* Watergate elided our trust in the absolute
authority of public discourse. *Blah, blah, blah.*

Simplify, simplify, simplify, says Thoreau.
*Inverted syntax. Run in fear of abstraction.*
Nixon's five o'clock shadow is insufficient cause
to eliminate theopenspacebetweenwords.
*Rethink the weak title. Risk something, man.*
Read Rilke's elegies in bed tonight.
*Show, don't tell.* Come see me during
Tuesday's office hour. *Show, don't tell.*
Marketing's your major, right? *Awk.*
Don't despair. *There's a poem in here somewhere.*

interesting style / form

# How He Answered the Glossy Magazine's
## *Mate-Poaching* Survey

*Rate how frequently the following tactics have been employed to
attract you as a short-term partner (i.e., one-night stand) when
you were already in a romantic relationship with another. Use this
sliding scale: Never/Once/Sometimes/Occasionally/Often/Always.*

Sometimes she wore black spandex and Jogbra
for no apparent reason. Occasionally she played golf,
never in my foursome. Often she pointed out
my girlfriend's bad grammar, bad breath, big rear.
Once, while I napped, she alphabetized my CDs.
At lunch, she sometimes peeled my banana.
Occasionally she endeared herself to my peers
by smoking cigars and tossing back Jack Daniels.
Always she bought the shots of Jack.
Sometimes she begged for Central High football stories.
Once she asked if I played Tight End. Never did she giggle.
Always she drank from an always-pink straw.
Sometimes she mowed my grass, waxed my Jeep,
scrubbed the tub. Once she cried during *Patton*.
She baked lasagna with meat. Always with meat.
Once she asked me to fill her heated water bed.
She often called about business then switched topics
to the '75 Reds. Sometimes she called me Charlie Hustle.
Once she pitted cherries wearing only a white tee shirt.
Often she introduced my mate to someone else, say,
my CEO who drives a Jag. She never liked Marge Schott.
On Halloween she always wore seductive costumes:
a *Playboy* bunny suit, pajamas with feet and crotch flap,
Saran Wrap accented with pitted cherries.

*Anaphora*

Once she invited me to her Super Bowl party
and quoted Bradshaw's pregame analysis. Howie's, too.
Once she challenged my partner to a front yard fight.
Never did she try to be my best friend.
Occasionally she called me her Big Red Machine.
Once she pitted cherries while I watched.

# Upon Blowing Our Chance to Meet the
# Poet Laureate, Who's Probably a Nice Guy

Deb and I'd made the cut for the *Post-Poetry-Reading Party,*
        a phrase that implies poetry, like Nietzsche's god,
is dead. This then must've been poetry's pitiable wake—
        a plethora of black and the stereo's dirigible solo
played so low everyone's splayed yoga-style.

Make no mistake, we were happy to be there, relegated
        to the kitchen where wine's uncorked, beer's imported,
and the scotch is both blended and not. Careful not to spill
or double-dip a chip, nearly home free amidst
the room's besotted careerism, we'd only to pass Question B

of the literary party-pack our host bought to enliven festivities:
        "Which of your books or albums most embarrasses you?"
Good question. The host purrs for her it's *Old Possum's Book of Cats,*
        or Cleveland Symphony's limping Beethoven, the sorry
guest conductor afflicted with gout. Harrumphs all around.

We wondered what's safer: Barry White's *Greatest Hits*
        or Rod McKuen's voice recording *Home to the Sea,*
the husky whisper that earned his first poet's million.
        Instead we chanced our Monkees albums—America's pre-MTV
made-to-order boy band, and Fate's three hags snipped our thread.

44

Our host's eyes saucered beneath her brow's highbrow arch,
      but we offered how Davey grew cuter, Mickey more zany,
and Peter thumbed his bass as if for real while the TV show spun
      its groove around Mike of sideburns and stocking cap,
who'd get rich years hence when his mommy invents Liquid Paper.

The humor was slapstick, their musical interludes improbable
      as those Bing and Bob concocted to appease the WWII
homefront, but this time it's Vietnam, a moral quandary,
      so the guys' striped bellbottoms and polka-dotted poets' shirts
implied ambivalence toward the military industrial complex.

The best of us hated them. The best of us wanted to be them.
      That's why we hated ourselves. Listen, we'd heard "I'm a Believer"
and yearned to be one. With Watts, Newark, Detroit aflame,
      RFK and MLK shot dead, with Tet's pistol
at our temple, who'd not prefer Camelot's ransacked castle?

*Click,* it's over. Though no one had yet invented the TV remote,
      they're as past tense as innocence. *Click, click.* — onomatopoeia
Even Jimi Hendrix, his Afro a black cloud, opened seven times   metaphor
      for the Monkees when the boys dared a live tour,
and then he'd had enough. Plucking the guitar with his teeth,

he flipped off a white bread crowd and thus fingered the button
      of his own destruction. Our Whitman in paisley,
he doused his Fender with lighter fluid, a soul sacrifice, then thrust
      its flames in his crotch. *Right on,* we yawped, *far out!*
"Oh," the host replied, shifting her ample slip, "Oh, good heavens."

# Etiquette and Epiphany in the Post-Workshop Men's Room

Urinal Rule #1 advises: Look Straight Ahead,
a precept slyly violated so I might spy the Sikh's
tufted burgundy turban cinched by a hidden knife.
The good news was he'd not dawdle at the sink,
brushing wisps across his thinning crown.
His lifelong hair was swaddled in silk.
In this fashion, braided as well as armed,
he'll depart our world dressed to fight or be forgiven.
Rule #2 warns: Shake It Only Twice.
I've not carried a weapon into some forlorn workshop,
happier still my students weren't packing.
Poetry unwinds even the tightest turban
and finds there its surreptitious knife.
*Here, it hurts here,* some poets say, begging
to be nailed to a cross of their own making.
Rule #3 urges: Always Wash Your Hands.
On Friday I feel like Pilate, condemning students
with red ink and terminal comments, but it's the story
of Jesus' washing his disciples' feet I love most,
how they squirmed to have The Boss scrub their toes.
Rule #4 suggests: Stand Two Urinals Apart.
Because Brother Mary walked his bike to workshop,
I thought this a penance and passed him twice
on some errand or another, though not thrice
as the cock's crow once betrayed.
Have you ever seen a monk lift his gown to pee?
At the porcelain urinal he held his
like a guy forgiving the knife that's killing him.

I wondered what hurts worse: refusing women
or their refusing you. I asked, no, not that,
but would he like a ride. Brother Mary—
who'd married Jesus, whose pantoum rhymed
*Lord* and *turd,* whose grade was pass/fail—
slung his Schwinn in my Honda's trunk
and looped a rosary to tie it shut.
Wait. Aren't we all pass/fail?
Rule #5: Last One Out, Turn Off the Light.

# The Other One

*Books in Print* attests I'm doppelganged by another
Kevin Stein, whose quill pens tales of dragons,
magic castles, and sorcerers tapping wands
both good and evil. There's the usual slew
of potions, spells, and curses cured by a kiss.
A few heaving bosoms and menace masquerading
as an apple. Please don't sue me, Mr. Stein.
For reasons I only imagine, he calls himself
"The Man in Black." When Amazon.com lists
his damsel and dragons beside mine, I cringe.
No doubt he's creeped out by my buntings,
race riots, and the too thin deaf man
with lopped-off hands. Egads.
People buy his book online thinking it's mine.
Maybe they're the folks who wrote the *Journal Star*
to pledge my soul to hell and urge the Bishop
quick excommunicate that heathen. Still,
think of the slothful Goth who glosses
a book's blurbs and gets mine instead of his.
What curses? What laughter among the coven?
Like most writers, we're guilty of solipsism,
wasting gallons of coffee to pry the other's
daffy tar-baby from our serious pink palms.
"Oh, the work's my life," we squeal. Well yes,
and no. Poetry exposes the soul's leitmotif,
but life's a messy cauldron of bliss and traffic tickets.
The two of us are bound as in marriage. Our name's
the vow, and neither church nor state will sunder

48

what our parents joined by chance. Anyway,
he's probably a swell guy. If we were to meet,
we'd shake, "Hi, I'm Kevin Stein." Then what?
Beck's and a Guinness—he's German-Irish too.
Then photos of my kids and his black cats,
chit chat and weather, the unenlightened presses,
and by the way, how his books sell more than mine.

# To Bob Marley's Toe

You killed him when bullets couldn't.
        Nor could white politicos,
                nor Brits with handouts, handcuffs
        the Marxists and Colonials had up their sleeves.
Nor black jealousy nor black pride,
                Haile's movement
        and all those spliffs up in smoke.
You slew when neither lungs
                nor throat would,
        nor voice like mangoes in moonlight,
fruit so sweet its split husk
                grants ants their share.
When neither Trenchtown
                nor its horrid porridge
        could do him in,
nor fear's carriage he pushed on through,
                you killed him killed.
Did you envy his dreads,
        or was it the lips revolt was sung from?
Were you bitter, imprisoned against his sandal's sole,
        while he freed others?
What of songs you propped up—
        work, after all, you pointed the way for!
*This way,* you nodded,
                though who noticed you?
                        You, who bore the cancer.

Ah, by hook of crooked foot
        you plotted to haul
  the great man down,
        thorn in the lion's paw. *metaphor*
You who tapped the beat
    *irony*  of his redemption song.

# Ghosts

My friend, referring to himself in third person,
claims another guy writes his poems, though
most times he's the other guy. Knowing the self
is thus a trick of purchase as costly as my new boots,
and there's only blisters to say about that.
Experience shows people get blisters
from the ill-fitted or from hard work,
but some work that's hard is also ill-fitting.
Have you ever graded thirty-two freshman essays?
Perhaps one needs a ghostwriter to be short-listed,
a name upon the tongue. Have I mentioned my new boots?
It's an attention problem really. In that regard,
its twin pleasures mimic chocolate mint and good sex—
the one makes you fat, which you better not get
if you want any of the other. When there's static
on the car radio, hearing every third word
makes Rush make sense, a tactic surrealists use
to decode the infinite metanarrative,
though it always ends with the Frisbee
in a cat's mouth. Touch it, and you'll get bit.
My friend says, "Never bite the hand that needs you,"
or is it, "Never kiss a gift-horse"? Pay attention!
My daughter's bay mare won National Top Ten,
so any day she'll demand a ghost rider
for her sore back. "Pay attention," she whinnies,
snuffling her ribbons and roses to remind herself
who she is. In this way her need bewilders
as does mine each morning—a ghost

wavering in the bathroom's foggy mirror,
this intimate stranger. Who, me? Pronouns
are so transparent everyone sees through them,
and there's all that chain jangling anyway.
'Fess up. *I* is a spook, a floating apparition,
the invisible Frisbee in a cat's mouth.
*Drop,* one commands, but cats never listen.

# To Bananas

They defame you who say we go bananas
when monkeying around. It's not fool's gold
that rises in us as yellow does in you.
It's 14 karat that can't be banked and must
be spent as you must be eaten now
or go to mush by noon. Who has time
to bake you into bread, anyway?
Donovan sang the '60s "Mellow Yellow"
and everyone baked your peel in ovens
hoping to find that starry celestial dynamo
in their dilated eyes and for once I said no.
I like you with milk and Wheaties, reading
the pictured sports hero's life story
that always includes a wholesome breakfast
not to mention twelve-hour training days.
I like to watch a beautiful woman peel
and eat you slowly, with conviction,
though in public I have to break you
into little pieces that aren't so phallic.
You've loads of potassium, which helps
in cases of *Giardia,* the bug I cupped up
from a Rockies stream. My diet: you,
white rice, water—so pure it seemed to
wash away as well my indiscretions.
What's sweet but problematic is how
delicate you are. Always bruised by lunch,
you can forget about suitcase or airplane!
Wounded as you, cheerleaders, bah,

they never noticed but once and thus
see "indiscretions" above, thank you.
I miss Chiquita banana girl who raised me
as a boy. No, it wasn't you in my pocket
but her I was happy to see. Today I bought
a wooden prop with polished hook for you
to ripen on. My friend Tomas claims
in America we never get your tastiest cousins,
exotic ones, though I've hung in a tree like you
and fallen too, but never into anyone's arms.

# Reliquary

*- A receptacle for keeping or displaying sacred relics*

In the news photo she pinches a frozen, Saran-wrapped
    catfish fillet
between her index finger and thumb, the way priests hold
    the communion wafer—
reverently, secretly giddy, alive with the apparition that
    he too lives,
the son who died but did not arise three days after
    reeling this fish
from the muddy Illinois, her boy gone fifteen years.
    But not.
"This, last thing he touched alive in the world," she sighs,
    shorthand
for the car wreck, the phone call, how she never got to
    say goodbye.
*imagery*   This yellowed, freezer-burned, power outage-thawed
    relic.

She looms stricken and unguarded in the half-page
    full-color shot,
slow news Sunday, wearing her best polyester top
    and matching slacks,
gold lamé elastic slippers. Her bouffant's lacquered stiff
    for the photographer
who arrived late and drunk, certain his career bottomed
    on this catfish fillet.
That's his joke, though not the one I'd waited for,
    asking

irony to spike the postmodern punch, our hee-haw
    reprieve.
When I spied the photo's green-eyed kitty, Fate's Tabby,
    stretching
his claws toward the treasured fish, suddenly she's
    everyone's mother.

# Four

# Thinking of Kandinsky while Shaving My Father

It pains the back, not to mention the spirit,
to kneel beside one's father limp in his electric lift chair.
Scrape goes the blade, tick the clock whose arms
spin blades pinned at the donkey's tail
heart makes of us. With one deft false move

I could end this, though try that excuse on the cops.
Next his hair cut and shampoo, my day's dirty work
spiraled down the drain. Who's weak now?
For scenes like these, Kandinsky claims
the spirit can be strengthened by exercise.

Because the soul's no muscle, it's not the sub-
four-minute Nicene Creed he's after, but his painting's
"blue brake on yellow resulting in green temporarily paralyzed"—
which, once framed, makes inveigling beauty.
How to say such things in words?

When I shave my father, his head droops
deasil and widdershins, tick tock my hand print
red across his forehead. Hold still. Sit up.
He slumps when sleeping and not. There now,
it's a confessional poem. Am I happy?

If so, I'm yellow, says Kandinsky's theory of color,
manic as autumn's prodigal expansion in maple and elm,
oak tinged with red and these raised trumpets.
On the page white and black speak
the second great antithesis. We know the first.

The painter says this results from feeling
not from exact science. Then let me get it right,
or kneel upon the razor's never. Once he laid steamed cloth
upon my cheeks. He lathered my pink face.
Now he shows me how to die.

In some cultures the son quaffs stump water.
In some cultures they build rafts and set father aflame
on his midnight river, even if there's no clock.
Come morning there's feeling but not exact science.
Come morning there's ash, a burnt log or two,

the blue heron lifting off at first light.

# Theory & Practice

Whenever I find my mother baking a cake,
    I know someone's dead. After the funeral mass,
her angel's food soon sweetens bereaved lips.
        Lévi-Strauss thought artists "shape the beautiful

and useful out of the dump heap of human life."
    He called it *bricolage:* using "whatever comes to hand."
In this way the cook who's magic with leftovers
        practices culinary bricolage, and a nerd cobbling

together computer parts exhibits technical bricolage.
    So the poet of apples and oranges makes what?
Fruit salad? Or should I take solace in
        Heraclitus's claim, "The fairest order is a heap

of random sweepings"? Perhaps, though remember
    he thinks the ways up and down are one!
Which theory explains what I make of
        my mother's baking? Let me start again.

When I was a boy, she peddled cakes and pies
    to pay the week's grocery bill. White-gloved
ladies rang our bell but didn't come in. By then,
        one's read enough to know what *urchin* means.

Now she works the church's Funeral Baking Committee,
    doling her dished and sugared condolences
to kids of former customers. Do they taste
    that taste and ponder their dead parents?

Archilochus contends, "The fox knows many things,
    the hedgehog only one. One big one."
Am I the hedgehog? Am I blind?
    Try this: "Wisdom," Heraclitus theorizes,

"understands the thought that steers all things,"
    his way of praising in theory, well, covert *Logos*—
the invisible cosmic order. In practice it goes
    like this: What my mother baked went quick out

the door to cool upon the seats of Cadillacs.
    One lady offered me a tip, not the usual nickel:
"Boy, remember your place. What you smell,
    you'll never taste." Hers was devil's food.

# Valentine's Day Boxing at the Madison County Jail

## I

How not to think of the end when beginning such a keen
   teenage plea,
the languorous roll of language off your tongue's slow spindle,
   the pauses
and aptly crafted balance of seriousness and humor that features
   the eyes,
ah, the eyes to distract from a hand's task unbuttoning this
   or unzipping that,
all of it timed to the exquisite crescendo of a planned last line:
   say, three words,
a sentence whose goal is nothing less than the bliss of acquiescence,
   the pyrotechnic ka-boom
that follows *yes.* (This, the exact tactic I'd already used, except
   for the sex part,
to seduce the public school system, where three polysyllabics
   and one
choice semicolon earned not merely an *A* but also a flush
   of scholarship cash.
How they loved the noble, working poor!) In the Age of Aquarius
   her happy planet
converged with mine in a TV-lit room, at the exact instant
   her doting father,
county Sheriff, fifth degree black belt in judo *and* karate,
   his chest
as broad as the Magnavox console whose flickerings we necked by,
   opened

the family room door on us. She was, of course, a knockout,
    blonde hair
waterfalling down her lithe back, and thus worth the risk
    splayed there
on the red plaid couch of the Sheriff's quarters fronting the jail,
    where they lived
in shag rug opulence, including the requisite drooling French poodle.

## II

Among the ramshackle and triple-locked homes of Madison Avenue,
    irony no one got,
Reggie played sole proprietor of a hair boutique, a role that in 1972,
    Year of The Big Hair,
meant Afro Sheen and straightener for the ladies, huge handled combs
    and plastic picks
for the brothers' massive Afro that Huey and the gang looked bad in—
    meaning good;
meaning don't mess with me, man; meaning Black Power—
    meaning too that Reggie
made his money not on cuts but on accessories and the doobie dealt
    from his back room
that emptied on a cinder alley, until the off-duty cop eyed the daffy
    laughing crowd
and that was the blunt end of that. For this, he pulled down
    six months,
lucky that Joe Buck, The Hanging Judge, was doing Vegas and
    the week's replacement
was a Dem soft on weed. Hand-quick and pitiless, a flawless
    Army middle-weight,
he'd boxed his plane ride out of Nam, and won a dozen pro bouts
    at the Indianapolis Armory
where Marvelous Marvin Johnson was gilding his nickname.
    Three months in,

Reggie earned "trustee," and the Sheriff strung ropes and posts
    around his judo mats
so Reggie had a ring to work out in. He'd pummeled his way
    through the jailhouse—
big ones, fat ones, edgy guys with scars. No deputy would risk
    his reputation.
On Valentine's Day, it thus came to pass that the red-faced Sheriff
    jerked me
by the scruff of my pencil neck up the steps to the attic ring
    where Reggie and I,
in service of our mutual rehabilitation, were bade go at it.

## III

Resplendent in black silk, he must've hated me, goose-bumped
    and blotchy
in the loaned, oversized trunks. Hated the scholarship kid
    and budding poet
from white-trashville blacks wouldn't drive through for fear
    of a tossed bottle,
the shot. I'd have hated me too. Slipping on his right glove,
    he whistled
Mississippi spring, his Aunt dusting white folks' fine china,
    Uncle Ned dead
at Da Nang. With the left came Martin, Medgar, and RFK,
    who didn't act rich.
The thumb of each he reserved for poking boys' blue eyes.
    Mine were green.
And green in the ring, too: that sweat-stained, ill-fitting headgear,
    a chewed-on mouthpiece—
how many had spit through this?—the bell's cranked clunk
    and ding.
He must've hated his predicament: How to thump the Sheriff's
    future son-in-law?

Too much and your black ass is back in isolation. Too little
    and it's February's
red-striped road crew. Must've hated Cupid's sorry arrow and naked
    pink fanny—
like Santa and Jesus, Cupid's always white. Hated the proverbial blonde,
    John Law's daughter,
palms against cheeks he'd never get to nuzzle, her puzzled contrite eyes
    watery
as the country club pools he'd cleaned one incessant summer.

## IV

If you're white in America—thus twice blessed—race is an ocean
    you sail clear of,
the way those old maps, whose ignorance we trusted, warned us
    *Here Be Dragons.*
Fire-breathing, cross-burning, Watts-aflame dragons, ugly as
    the mirrored face
you won't claim. Not yours, its curses not yours. Dare I say
    what *I* was thinking
as he sliced and diced my melon head? That over beer and his
    reefers
the two of us would feed our munchies, hum a little Motown?
    Fooled you,
dear gullible reader. No, once in a clench, both wet with sweat,
    when my forehead lay against
the nap—yes, the nap—of his hair, his against my stringy mop,
    he'd told me,
"Your hair stinks like a wet dog," and I'd replied, "Yours feels like
    a Brillo pad."
Neither of us laughed, though after that I was Doggie and he Brillo.

# V

Sure I'm telling on myself as if to expunge some guilt Freud might
    make sense of.
Or St. Augustine. Or maybe Malcom X. As if the page were couch.
    Tired of his toy,
Reggie measured me with outstretched left, laid Martin and Medgar
    atop
my head, then right-crossed me out. Good night, wan prince.
    His fists,
of course, resolved nothing. In a month she and I were back at it,
    this time
in my blue Chevy a deputy flashed his lights so brightly in
    her daddy shotgunned
our engagement. Reggie unlocked his boarded-up shop,
    but cops
circled its uninhabited planet like white moons gone mad,
    so even
upright clientele veered like comets from the nightstick's gravity.
    I'd ringside seats
for Reggie's next win, but he weak-kneed three straight losses,
    and Indy's
swollen lips first kissed then swallowed him like blood.
    Come July,
after the usual fireworks, I drove him home to sit in front of
    not *in*
his house because, he apologized, his sister was "prejudiced."
    It was Mogen David,
cheap and unconsecrated, but the wine got us where we wanted
    to go—
beyond the screened porch of his white house, high above the sky
    sprawled
below us, stars in our eyes we didn't give or take a punch to see.

# Found in a Shoe Box Labeled "Keep"

I.

Herman Stein Writes Cpl. Everett Stein, U.S. Army
*31 August 1918*

You ascked that I may send you a few lines
in my hand, son. I hope these will not try
your head, my words worse mispelled
than your last, you now three years out of skul.

I will tell you we are allways glad to hear
from you, and that most I leave this
writing to mother, our secratary at home,
and to sister Agnes, herself ten years out of skul.

I never forget you anyday in my prayer.
When I work my mums, they bloom
white for you. All the times I was glad to hear
a Soldeers life appeals to you. No mispelled

lettur lessons your duty and the hardships
I honor you for. I am also glad to lurn
you are promoted to Corporal, and as you
have wit and talent enough, you should try

to bring it to Sargent. Not for better pay
but for the honor also, and for the futur.
Yours. I am sick with a bruced knee,
and so when you ascked for a few lines

you get them from bed. My bumped knee
has swollen and the doctor has bed rest
and flaxseed poulters on it. No blood poisen
or stiffness has come of it, but these lines

have oshun and waves in them like those
you crossed back over. I thought our family
done with those cold waters, and with Germany.
Shipped to France, your brother Joe will try

to find Leo in all that mud. With Job we say:
the Lord giveth, the Lord taketh away.
If the Berlin train is not blown up, take the run
to Salzbergen, where Aunt Trilling will spell

your hardships with a kiss. These few lines
asck God to bless you in field and trench. Oh, try
not to shoot your cousens. Have I mispelled?
You boys are but a few years out of skul.

## 2.

Trilling Writes Her Brother Herman in America
*Salzbergen, Germany, 14 January 1935*

Dear brother, many say it could come to war again.
The days dawn black as coal and hot with fire
from throats of little brown men with hearts of tin.
You know from your newspapers how things conspire

to make days dawn black as coal and hot with fire.
Many here are sickly because of unhealthy weather.
You know from your newspapers how things conspire.
It freezes for a couple days and we get better,

though many here are sickly because of the weather.
We haven't had winter, no pink cheeks or snow.
It freezes for a couple of days and we get better.
No one starves much any more. Food grows under our toes.

We haven't had a winter, no pink cheeks or snow.
Brother Gerhard says he eats enough but other things go bad.
No one starves much any more. Food grows around our toes,
for we've spiced soup with old shoe leather. Don't gag.

Brother Gerhard says he eats enough but other things go bad.
Elizabeth Gronefeld suffered cancer of the hand and died
just after dinner soup spiced with shoe leather. Don't gag.
In poverty she sickened so quick her finger fell off while she bathed.

Did I write how Elizabeth had cancer, oh yes, and died?
Her boys went down in the Great War. Our daughters married drunks.
Elizabeth sickened so quick her finger fell off while she bathed.
I'd like to send you new year blessings, but my heart's sunk.

All the good boys died in the war. Our daughters married drunks
who limp, smoke too much, and curse the mustard gas.
I'd like to send you new year blessings, but my heart's sunk.
If you were here, your sister Trilling would crawl to Sunday Mass.

Our streets fester with old soldiers who curse the mustard gas.
My name in English, you say, is like a bird's sappy song.
If you were here, I would kneel all through Sunday Mass.
"Trilling" is what birds do when they're happy.

My name in English sounds like a bird's sappy song.
You know from the newspapers how fire heats hearts of tin.
"Trilling" is what birds do when they're happy.
Dear brother, many say it could come to war again.

# In the Nuclear Age

So, reader, forget for a moment the missile treaty
just revoked. Forget *throw weight* and *sunshine units*
and the various MIRV technologies China stole.
Oh middle-aged, forget how you squatted beneath
the wooden school desk, hands over your empty head.

Jam to the song Suzy and Bob jam to,
circa 1969, as she unlocks daddy's bomb shelter
and lays him gentle down beside Caterpillar generators
vented to the surface. Hum the dirge
that soundtracks my generation's Chartres.

Dig how Black Sabbath's "Paranoid" electrifies
as improbably as Khrushchev's shoe thumping
the podium, the heel threatening to "bury" us.
Yeah, buddy?! There's NORAD, SAC, ICBMs,
a halo of silos, and if all else fails, the shelter's

dank belly delivering post-holocaust afterlife:
water tins, saltines, a Swiss army knife.
And when the Death-Box becomes Love-Shack,
there's Marvin Gaye's "What's Going On."
Boogie down so its mix of politics and sex cements

the surest bomb shelter. Screw you, Khrushchev—
Suzy and Bob believe brother Marvin's mojo:
*War is not the answer. Only love can conquer hate.*
So they cut the Hot Line in fevered quest of
Mutually Assured Destruction, an orgasm frothing

the sea Cronus populated with sperm whales,
angelfish, and the first salamander who'll plop on land
to evolve, Darwin postulates, into daddy home early.
Suzy's, in fact, who finds his Doberman barking
at the shelter door, a box not unlike Pandora's.

Now, now, could their story end otherwise?
After all, Marvin's father shoots him dead in a fit
of paranoia, ecstatic or not. There's no escaping
The Man. Who'd choose to be the last,
the nestled unforgiven? Who'd embrace erasure—?

all that nothing yours alone.

# Upon Freeing the Ruby-Throated Hummingbird Beak-Stuck in a Screen Door

There's cresting Quandary Peak, oh mountain
of the human condition. There's Mt. of the Holy Cross
roped in rain and fog so thick we missed
the glacial cross Longfellow's sonnet made famous
for a slim generation's attention span. There's
summiting Mt. Elbert when Deb was pregnant,
our daughter bagging her first peak *in utero,*
or was it weeks before when part of us crossed

over to her? Those times I rose above
some other worldly body. I stood at the edge,
still do, my breath fast and shallow,
nose pressed against the thin scrim
that gives a little and thus gives nothing,
oh scrim between the known and not,
oh lousy metaphor for death—
this a problem and the beauty we inhabit,
or do I mean embody?

Look, he hung there, my brother, beak-stuck
and sun-stroked, begging one more chance,
anthem of those who sigh *Oh* way too often.
He'd nearly crossed over but to what?
Plucked free, he feasted on sugar water,
iridescent electric trembling, pilgrim and homeboy.
And what of his crested moments?
There's trumpet flower till its red throat wilts silent.

There's monkshood till it folds to seeds' reprieve—
how these things we love add up, oh tweedle dee,
as they count down.

# To Wheelbarrows

You, whom Dr. Williams depends upon
beside the white chickens.
And the big one I grunted full of shingles
uphill to a bin, until nails pierced your twin tires
and I'd Sisyphus push no more.
You in whom I learned desire's physics
when Paula modeled how her bandanna might in a pinch,
say, on some desert isle, serve ably as a blouse.
Or nearly so.
You, stenciled Property of Gabbert Construction,
loaded with bricks Mexicans muscled up planks,
their legs brown pistons chugging hod
to the engine we capitalists call *labor* if it's others' sweat
and *work* if it's ours.
What pleasure is there for you,
rusted Sears brand full of crushed Pabst cans?
Hard by Kickapoo Creek,
hard by the bonfire men drink by,
hard men who glower in drivers' eyes.
Come rain then snow, men with cans in hand
and you there, full of empties. You, heaped heartache.
What answers your despair?
Only you, Old Red, *my* wheelbarrow
in whom I lugged limestone
but also raced the kids around our yard,
until a spin that split Joseph's lip and spilled his
the color of you. In whom I learned, again,
never mix work with pleasure.

In whom I hauled grandma's grass clippings
to earn the martyr Kennedy's fifty-cent piece
saved so long in my underwear drawer
all of us are ratty, or dead.
Only you at dusk in garden muck.
Only you, in whom the bay mare's droppings
blaze orange with fire,
as if piety might yet flare in me.

# While Writing This Poem, My Horse Jumped the Pasture Fence

My title's dangling modifier creates
ambiguity and perhaps humor.
But isn't syntax, like a joke, all timing?
Okay, death can mean being in the wrong place
at the right time, but mostly it's just time.
Saying something's misplaced implies
a right place I'm not sure of,
which implies as well wanting to believe,
so go ahead and make fun of that. Belief's
what one gets dangling over a cliff. Aren't we?

What I mean is my mare's jumped the fence
and gone, but *gone* means she's waiting
by the stable not the gone my father was. Or is.
Still, what's perfectly out of place evokes laughter,
as when the agency's Rod Stewart impersonator
drunkenly shows up for the kids' Meet Santa Day
and "Maggie May" gives way to "A Reason to Believe"
just as St. Nick hops off his Harley to high-five
faux Rod who gets paid anyway. In this manner
luck implies beneficent misplacement, though beware
the med-school gasser: *As soon as completely anesthetized,*
*you may begin the patient's lateral abdominal incision.*

*Tick tock.* Once a poet friend sold shoes, the gamut
from little kicky things to work boots. She'd fold
her poems *tick* in shoe boxes, curling sonnets *tock*
amidst the Birkenstocks, pantoums prim in black pumps.

Imagine the pedestrian *tick tock* solaced by assonance,
the practical and extravagant bedded down—if only
for the ride home. The ride home's how I imagine
heaven, only never getting there. In this way I love
our cherry tree *tick tock* off kilter: what beetles did,
how bag worms and farmland chemical drift rifted
all but one arthritic branch, scraggly but cupped enough
for the single cardinal double-red as a cherry
upon your tongue. In this way I loved my *tick tock* father's
corkscrewed finger, how he pitched a handsome curve

and rolled the bowler's natural hook, his bent pinkie
last I saw and nearly touched but the casket clunked shut.
It's time's disarray we're victims and agents of.
Try this: *As a young boy, his mother told stories of her year
as a country schoolmarm.* No, what I mean is
his right eye loomed bluer than his left.
What I mean is I love skewed beauty, misplaced
and amazed as lupine zigzagging the mailman's path
to my porch steps. What to say of that?
Dangle this: Abloom here and there amidst
the brick walk, my father's eyes sway lupine blue.

# These Gifts

Alone I spied the barred owl hard against
    the moon's cleft side. From claw to ear,
his mottled body throttled then calmed,
    eyes wide with the *O* of joy.

Not *who?, who?, who?* but *owl, owlll, owwlll*
    he sang, as if some god had granted him
the answer. Sure, half-drunk with sleep,
    I envied him his certainty—he knew

who he was and had voice to sing it,
    like the Disney-types kids go crazy over,
talking Mickey in every bed. If animals
    could speak, what would they tell us of us?

In the dream I'd been awakened from, I lay
    on my deathbed circled by creatures I'd eaten
along the way: 11 cows, 32 pigs and sheep,
    85 turkeys, 2,570 chickens counting their eggs,

schooled cod and salmon from my Catholic tryst.
    This, the Nativity in reverse—
not a god coming in but a man going out,
    each one attended by creatures and gifts.

All the squawking, bleating, mooing, crapping.
　　All the hooves, scales, snouts, and feathered wings.
All the life I'd consumed to feed mine. Don't forget
　　bushels of wheat and rice, tomatoes that bleed

beneath the knife, cantaloupe so sweet its husk has split,
　　broccoli stalks steamed with butter.
We know the joke's punchline goes like this: Corn
　　has ears and potatoes eyes to hide from hungry us.

What then should I sing upon the bur oak branch?
　　I'd like to say I feel sorrow, though it's more
a forced remorse, some Edenic yearning
　　those fated gates slammed shut on. Bye, bye.

I'd like to say this guilt tastes of iron as blood does,
　　though what am I?—nothing, but a man.
These gifts I can't mourn. These gifts I lift
　　like prayer to my tongue. I eat beauty.

# Won't You Stand Next to My Fire

"Them's my hands," grinned the guy I tooled
cars with, showing off *Smith's Diesel Repair Manual*—
photos of hands cleaning valves, tempering
an ill-tempered crank shaft, oh anything
the "thinking man's manual for engine repair"
ought to proffer a shot of hands doing. Flushed
with oily fingers turning pages he'd starred on,
he planned life as the lone hand model
beloved in truck stops: Free beer and apple pie,
then the Lava soap commercial. Step # 1: Always
read Safety Instructions before *yadda yadda yadda.*
Step # 2: Insert Part A into Part B and twist
clockwise. Instead he stuck his paw
where the warning's "Never" had worn off.

Yes, the best made plans of mice and men go kaput,
but sometimes Disney comes of it. After his lawsuit,
the mechanic took early retirement and cut
filet mignon with his left. When life thus gives
you lemons, it's best to quaff the chocolate shake.
And though a stopped clock's right twice a day,
why look? What's catching you is you!
Once in Albuquerque, I misspelled *mispelling* seven times
grading a hazy legalization of *marijuanna* research paper,
so I called it even and gave the kid a B. Once
in Albu-whatever the 24–hour Beef Jerky Hut
went belly up, so an artist hauled its steroidal

fiberglass bull down Route 66 to where his heifers
waited in pasture, all their neon parts aglow.

Who imagined the Guggenheim so enamored
of bovine art? Who knew Chicago "udderly bonkers"
for painted cows? Chance can be genius in disguise.
Ask Indiana's radical feminists who ballpeened Adam's
bronze penis while giving statuesque Eve a spit shine,
performance art the NEA funded in bunches. Sure,
some guys use theirs with all the subtlety of a hammer,
though research shows roses and acoustic guitar
statistically more successful. Some guys, like Prometheus,
think everything's better with fire. So Jimi Hendrix
set his aflame, a Fender Stratocaster he bequeathed
to Frank Zappa then promptly died. Unabashed,
Zappa recorded *Zoot Allures* with the charred guitar
before prostate cancer hammered his private parts.

Jimi, when in the course of human events you spark fire,
give it plenty of air. When we the people take a hammer
to bronze, it'll just dent until brittle then piddle off.
When Zappa replaced the strings and a couple pickups,
Hendrix's Stratocaster peeled lead paint from schoolroom walls.
Not everything's fixable, but then again
not everything's broken. In this take heart.

# Tract

This poem's subject is the cantaloupe tilting
its burnished head in the garden's black dirt.
Its sensuous tumescence. Its musky scent.
This poem does not give a gnat's whit about
tomatoes the learned once called "love apples."
This poem's subject is the ripening cantaloupe.
This poem does not rely on catalog, nor does
it switch topics unrelentingly. This poem
esteems the cantaloupe, from Italian *Cantalupo,*
papal village near Rome where the good pontiff
prayed hard for the seed to take hold. This poem
eyes the cantaloupe's spritz of dew first glisten
then vanish, its veined skin blush as sun comes on.
This poem has no particular interest in the watermelon
whose belly plunks *not yet* beneath a hand's tap.
This poem's subject is the ripening cantaloupe,
its fringed leaf and tendril corkscrewed around
the sweet pepper stalk as if around a little finger.
This poem bears no ill toward Cortland apples
hard as cats' hearts, nor the pears just assuming
their young breast shape, but this poem's subject
is the cantaloupe ripening in black dirt—a moment
so near its stem has begun to unbutton. This poem
won't employ simile to imply the process is like
a woman's ripening, when mind rushes its juices
through her body's flushed fruit. This poem
is not meditative. Reader, do not ponder what
it means to ripen, wane, and die. This poem's
subject is the cantaloupe ripening in black dirt.

Kevin Stein is Poet Laureate of Illinois. He has authored seven books of poetry and criticism. Among his numerous honors are fellowships granted by the National Endowment for the Arts and the Illinois Arts Council, the Frederick Bock Prize awarded by *Poetry,* the *Indiana Review* Poetry Prize, and the Vernon Louis Parrington Medal for Distinguished Writing. He is Professor of English at Bradley University.

# Illinois Poetry Series
*Laurence Lieberman, Editor*

History Is Your Own Heartbeat
*Michael S. Harper* (1971)

The Foreclosure
*Richard Emil Braun* (1972)

The Scrawny Sonnets and
Other Narratives
*Robert Bagg* (1973)

The Creation Frame
*Phyllis Thompson* (1973)

To All Appearances:
Poems New and Selected
*Josephine Miles* (1974)

The Black Hawk Songs
*Michael Borich* (1975)

Nightmare Begins Responsibility
*Michael S. Harper* (1975)

The Wichita Poems
*Michael Van Walleghen* (1975)

Images of Kin: New and
Selected Poems
*Michael S. Harper* (1977)

Poems of the Two Worlds
*Frederick Morgan* (1977)

Cumberland Station
*Dave Smith* (1977)

Tracking
*Virginia R. Terris* (1977)

Riversongs
*Michael Anania* (1978)

On Earth as It Is
*Dan Masterson* (1978)

Coming to Terms
*Josephine Miles* (1979)

Death Mother and Other Poems
*Frederick Morgan* (1979)

Goshawk, Antelope
*Dave Smith* (1979)

Local Men
*James Whitehead* (1979)

Searching the Drowned Man
*Sydney Lea* (1980)

With Akhmatova at the Black Gates
*Stephen Berg* (1981)

Dream Flights
*Dave Smith* (1981)

More Trouble with the Obvious
*Michael Van Walleghen* (1981)

The American Book of the Dead
*Jim Barnes* (1982)

The Floating Candles
*Sydney Lea* (1982)

Northbook
*Frederick Morgan* (1982)

Collected Poems, 1930–83
*Josephine Miles* (1983; reissue, 1999)

The River Painter
*Emily Grosholz* (1984)

Healing Song for the Inner Ear
*Michael S. Harper* (1984)

The Passion of the
Right-Angled Man
*T. R. Hummer* (1984)

Dear John, Dear Coltrane
*Michael S. Harper* (1985)

Poems from the Sangamon
*John Knoepfle* (1985)

In It
*Stephen Berg* (1986)

The Ghosts of Who We Were
*Phyllis Thompson* (1986)

Moon in a Mason Jar
*Robert Wrigley* (1986)

Lower-Class Heresy
*T. R. Hummer* (1987)

Poems: New and Selected
*Frederick Morgan* (1987)

Furnace Harbor: A Rhapsody of the
North Country
*Philip D. Church* (1988)

Bad Girl, with Hawk
*Nance Van Winckel* (1988)

Blue Tango
*Michael Van Walleghen* (1989)

Eden
*Dennis Schmitz* (1989)

Waiting for Poppa at the
Smithtown Diner
*Peter Serchuk* (1990)

Great Blue
*Brendan Galvin* (1990)

What My Father Believed
*Robert Wrigley* (1991)

Something Grazes Our Hair
*S. J. Marks* (1991)

Walking the Blind Dog
*G. E. Murray* (1992)

The Sawdust War
*Jim Barnes* (1992)

The God of Indeterminacy
*Sandra McPherson* (1993)

Off-Season at the Edge of the World
*Debora Greger* (1994)

Counting the Black Angels
*Len Roberts* (1994)

Oblivion
*Stephen Berg* (1995)

To Us, All Flowers Are Roses
*Lorna Goodison* (1995)

Honorable Amendments
*Michael S. Harper* (1995)

Points of Departure
*Miller Williams* (1995)

Dance Script with Electric Ballerina
*Alice Fulton* (reissue, 1996)

To the Bone: New and
Selected Poems
*Sydney Lea* (1996)

Floating on Solitude
*Dave Smith* (3-volume reissue, 1996)

Bruised Paradise
*Kevin Stein* (1996)

Walt Whitman Bathing
*David Wagoner* (1996)

Rough Cut
*Thomas Swiss* (1997)

Paris
*Jim Barnes* (1997)

The Ways We Touch
*Miller Williams* (1997)

The Rooster Mask
*Henry Hart* (1998)

The Trouble-Making Finch
*Len Roberts* (1998)

Grazing
*Ira Sadoff* (1998)

Turn Thanks
*Lorna Goodison* (1999)

Traveling Light:
Collected and New Poems
*David Wagoner* (1999)

Some Jazz a While:
Collected Poems
*Miller Williams* (1999)

The Iron City
*John Bensko* (2000)

Songlines in Michaeltree:
New and Collected Poems
*Michael S. Harper* (2000)

Pursuit of a Wound
*Sydney Lea* (2000)

The Pebble: Old and New Poems
*Mairi MacInnes* (2000)

Chance Ransom
*Kevin Stein* (2000)

House of Poured-Out Waters
*Jane Mead* (2001)

The Silent Singer: New and
Selected Poems
*Len Roberts* (2001)

The Salt Hour
*J. P. White* (2001)

Guide to the Blue Tongue
*Virgil Suárez* (2002)

The House of Song
*David Wagoner* (2002)

X =
*Stephen Berg* (2002)

Arts of a Cold Sun
*G. E. Murray* (2003)

Barter
*Ira Sadoff* (2003)

The Hollow Log Lounge
*R. T. Smith* (2003)

In the Black Window: New and
Selected Poems
*Michael Van Walleghen* (2004)

A Deed to the Light
*Jeanne Murray Walker* (2004)

Controlling the Silver
*Lorna Goodison* (2005)

Good Morning and Good Night
*David Wagoner* (2005)

American Ghost Roses
*Kevin Stein* (2005)

## National Poetry Series

Eroding Witness
*Nathaniel Mackey* (1985)
Selected by Michael S. Harper

Palladium
*Alice Fulton* (1986)
Selected by Mark Strand

Cities in Motion
*Sylvia Moss* (1987)
Selected by Derek Walcott

The Hand of God and a Few
Bright Flowers
*William Olsen* (1988)
Selected by David Wagoner

The Great Bird of Love
*Paul Zimmer* (1989)
Selected by William Stafford

Stubborn
*Roland Flint* (1990)
Selected by Dave Smith

The Surface
*Laura Mullen* (1991)
Selected by C. K. Williams

The Dig
*Lynn Emanuel* (1992)
Selected by Gerald Stern

My Alexandria
*Mark Doty* (1993)
Selected by Philip Levine

The High Road to Taos
*Martin Edmunds* (1994)
Selected by Donald Hall

Theater of Animals
*Samn Stockwell* (1995)
Selected by Louise Glück

The Broken World
*Marcus Cafagña* (1996)
Selected by Yusef Komunyakaa

Nine Skies
*A. V. Christie* (1997)
Selected by Sandra McPherson

Lost Wax
*Heather Ramsdell* (1998)
Selected by James Tate

So Often the Pitcher Goes to
Water until It Breaks
*Rigoberto González* (1999)
Selected by Ai

Renunciation
*Corey Marks* (2000)
Selected by Philip Levine

Manderley
*Rebecca Wolff* (2001)
Selected by Robert Pinsky

Theory of Devolution
*David Groff* (2002)
Selected by Mark Doty

Rhythm and Booze
*Julie Kane* (2003)
Selected by Maxine Kumin

Shiva's Drum
*Stephen Cramer* (2004)
Selected by Grace Schulman

## Other Poetry Volumes

*Local Men* and *Domains*
*James Whitehead* (1987)

Her Soul beneath the Bone:
Women's Poetry on Breast Cancer
*Edited by Leatrice Lifshitz* (1988)

Days from a Dream Almanac
*Dennis Tedlock* (1990)

Working Classics: Poems on
Industrial Life
*Edited by Peter Oresick and
Nicholas Coles* (1990)

Hummers, Knucklers, and
Slow Curves: Contemporary
Baseball Poems
*Edited by Don Johnson* (1991)

The Double Reckoning of
Christopher Columbus
*Barbara Helfgott Hyett* (1992)

Selected Poems
*Jean Garrigue* (1992)

New and Selected Poems, 1962–92
*Laurence Lieberman* (1993)

*The Dig* and *Hotel Fiesta*
*Lynn Emanuel* (1994)

For a Living: The Poetry of Work
*Edited by Nicholas Coles and
Peter Oresick* (1995)

The Tracks We Leave: Poems on
Endangered Wildlife of North
America
*Barbara Helfgott Hyett* (1996)

Peasants Wake for Fellini's *Casanova*
and Other Poems
*Andrea Zanzotto; edited and
translated by John P. Welle and Ruth
Feldman; drawings by Federico Fellini
and Augusto Murer* (1997)

*Moon in a Mason Jar* and
*What My Father Believed*
*Robert Wrigley* (1997)

The Wild Card: Selected Poems,
Early and Late
*Karl Shapiro; edited by Stanley
Kunitz and David Ignatow* (1998)

*Turtle, Swan* and *Bethlehem in
Broad Daylight*
*Mark Doty* (2000)

Illinois Voices: An Anthology of
Twentieth-Century Poetry
*Edited by Kevin Stein and
G. E. Murray* (2001)

On a Wing of the Sun
*Jim Barnes* (3-volume reissue, 2001)

Poems
*William Carlos Williams; introduc-
tion by Virginia M. Wright-Peterson*
(2002)

Creole Echoes: The Francophone
Poetry of Nineteenth-Century
Louisiana
*Translated by Norman R. Shapiro;
introduction and notes by
M. Lynn Weiss* (2003)

Poetry from *Sojourner:*
A Feminist Anthology
*Edited by Ruth Lepson with Lynne
Yamaguchi; introduction by Mary
Loeffelholz* (2004)

Asian American Poetry:
The Next Generation
*Edited by Victoria M. Chang; fore-
word by Marilyn Chin* (2004)

Papermill: Poems, 1927–35
*Joseph Kalar; edited by Ted Genoways*
(2005)

UNIVERSITY OF ILLINOIS PRESS

1325 South Oak Street · Champaign, IL 61820-6903 · www.press.uillinois.edu